BEST OF
MEXICO

Consultant Editor:
Valerie Ferguson

HERMES
HOUSE

Contents

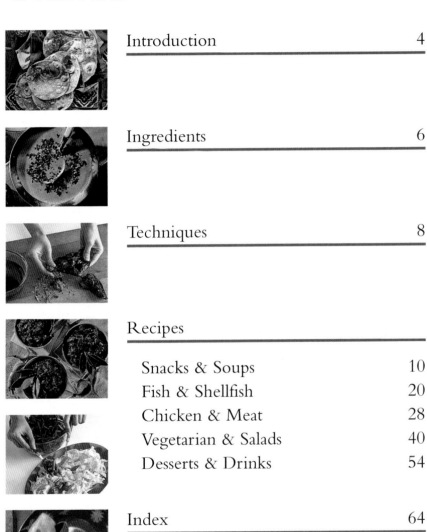

Introduction

Many of the foods we take for granted in the West were unknown before Christopher Columbus reached the Americas in 1492. The list is impressive. We had no corn (maize), tomatoes or peppers – sweet, pungent and hot – no beans, such as red kidney or pinto beans, no pumpkins or other winter squashes. Courgettes, avocados and guavas were equally unfamiliar, and we had never tasted chocolate or vanilla. Even turkeys were unknown.

All these foods originated in Mexico, where agriculture is believed to have been practised as long ago as 7,000 BC, about the same time, give or take a century or two, as the cultivation of food crops began in the Middle East.

The food of Mexico is strongly regional in character, featuring a wide variety of unique and delicious recipes. It is famous for its hot and spicy flavours and tomato-based sauces, although there are plenty more subtle dishes to try.

In *Best of Mexico* you will find a representative collection of the most celebrated dishes of this culinarily diverse country, from quick snacks such as Tacos and Tortillas to special occasion recipes including Veal in Sauce and Mole Poblano de Guajolote.

Ingredients

Mexico's temperate climate ensures it has a bounty of vegetables.

AVOCADOS

The avocado, which is now grown all over the world, originated in Central America. There are many recipes for the classic salsa, guacamole. In its simplest form it is made by mashing avocados with a squeeze or two of lemon or lime juice, a handful of chopped fresh coriander, a little crushed garlic, chopped spring onions, salt and chopped fresh serrano chillies.

BEANS

Dried beans (*frijoles*) are a Mexican staple, either served with a little cooking liquid, or mashed and fried as *refritos*. Pink, red and black haricot beans are native to Mexico, as are speckled pinto beans. Also popular are lima beans from Peru and fresh green beans.

CHILLIES AND PEPPERS

These are indigenous to Mexico and there are innumerable varieties. The most commonly used fresh green chillies are serrano, jalapeño and poblano, all hot. The habanero is small, flavourful and the hottest chilli in the world. It may be red or green and is used fresh. The most popular dried chillies are ancho (full-flavoured and mild) and chipotle (very hot). Other varieties include the mulato, which is pungent, and the hot pasilla. In addition there are the bell-shaped sweet peppers, otherwise known as capsicums. These may be green, yellow or red, depending on their ripeness, and they are not hot. Canned or bottled red peppers are called pimientos.

Clockwise from top left: dried chick peas, dried kidney beans, fresh green beans and dried pinto beans.

CHOCOLATE
Chocolate originated in Mexico thousands of years ago. It was drunk hot or cold, and foam-topped. Today it is sold in blocks flavoured with cinnamon, almonds and vanilla and is used in drinks and cooking.

CHORIZO
A highly seasoned, reddish-coloured link sausage much used in Mexican cooking. It comes in many varieties, but all contain pork and paprika, which gives them their distinctive colour.

CORIANDER
This fresh green feathery herb resembles Italian parsley or chervil in appearance and is widely used in Mexican cooking. The seeds are also used, but less extensively.

Clockwise from top centre: small green chillies, chipotle chillies, mulato chillies, habanero chillies, pasilla chillies, green peppers, green jalapeño chillies, anaheim chillies, and (centre left) Scotch Bonnet chillies, (centre right) fresh red chillies.

CORN (MAIZE)
Corn was one of the first plants cultivated in Mexico. The dried kernels are ground to make *masa harina* (dough flour), which is used to make tortillas and tamales.

TOMATILLOS (MEXICAN GREEN TOMATOES)
These are not unripe tomatoes, but come from a different plant. They are known as "husk tomatoes" because of their papery covering. Buy them in cans from specialist shops.

Techniques

PREPARING CHILLIES

1 Always protect your hands as chillies can irritate the skin; wear rubber gloves and never rub your eyes after handling chillies. Halve the chilli lengthways and remove and discard the fiery hot seeds.

2 Slice, finely chop and use the chillies as required. Wash the knife and chopping board thoroughly in hot, soapy water. Always wash your hands carefully after you have been preparing chillies.

PREPARING GARLIC

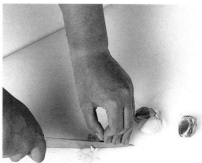

1 Break off the clove of garlic from the bulb, place the flat side of a large knife on top of the clove and strike it with your fist. Remove all the papery outer skin. Begin by finely chopping the clove.

2 Sprinkle over a little table salt and, using the flat side of a large knife blade, work the salt into the chopped garlic, until the clove softens and releases its aromatic juices. Use the garlic paste as required.

CHOPPING HERBS

1 Remove the leaves and place them on a clean, dry board. Use a large, sharp cook's knife (if you use a blunt knife you will bruise the herbs rather than chopping them) and chop them until as coarse or as fine as needed.

2 Alternatively, use a herb chopper, also called a mezzaluna, which is a very useful tool for finely chopping herbs or vegetables. Use a seesaw motion for best results.

PREPARING AVOCADOS

1 Use a sharp knife to cut around the centre of the avocado lengthways, to the large stone. Twist it to separate the halves, remove the stone, then use a spoon to scoop out the flesh into a mixing bowl.

2 Mash the avocado flesh thoroughly with a fork or a potato masher, or tip it out on to a board and chop finely, using a large knife. Use immediately, or the avocado will begin to discolour.

Corn Tortillas

Tortillas are easy to make using a tortilla press, which consists of two hinged circles of wood or metal.

Makes about 14 tortillas, 14 cm/5½ in diameter

INGREDIENTS
275 g/10 oz/2 cups *masa harina*
    (tortilla flour)
250–350 ml/8–12 fl oz/1–1½ cups water

1 Put the *masa harina* into a bowl and stir in 250 ml/8 fl oz/1 cup of the water, mixing to a soft dough that just holds together. If it is too dry, add a little more water. Cover the bowl with a cloth and set aside for 15 minutes.

2 Preheat the oven to 150°C/300°F/ Gas 2. Open the tortilla press and line both sides with a small plastic bag, cut open and halved crossways. Preheat a griddle until hot.

3 Knead the dough lightly and shape into 14 balls. Put a ball on the press and bring the top down firmly to flatten the dough out into a round.

4 Open the press, peel off the top layer of plastic and lift the tortilla by means of the bottom plastic. Turn it on to your palm, so that the plastic is uppermost. Peel off the plastic and flip the tortilla on to the hot griddle.

5 Cook for about 1 minute or until the edges start to curl. Turn over and cook for a further 1 minute. Wrap in foil and keep warm in the oven.

COOK'S TIP: Tortillas are very easy to make but it is important to get the dough texture right. If it is too dry and crumbly, add a little water; if it is too wet, add more *masa harina*. If you misjudge the pressure needed for flattening the ball of dough to a neat circle on the tortilla press, just scrape it off, re-roll it and try again.

Flour Tortillas

Make flour tortillas if *masa harina* is unavailable. To keep them soft and pliable, make sure they are kept warm.

Makes about 14 tortillas, 15 cm/6 in diameter

INGREDIENTS
225 g/8 oz/2 cups plain flour
5 ml/1 tsp salt
15 ml/1 tbsp lard or vegetable fat
120 ml/4 fl oz/½ cup water

1 Sift the flour and salt into a mixing bowl. Rub in the lard or vegetable fat with your fingertips until the mixture resembles coarse breadcrumbs.

2 Gradually add the water and mix to a soft dough. Knead lightly, form into a ball, cover the bowl with a cloth and leave to rest for 15 minutes.

3 Divide the dough into about 14 portions and form into balls. Roll out each ball of dough in turn on a lightly floured board to a round measuring about 15 cm/6 in. Trim the rounds if necessary.

4 Preheat the oven to 150°C/300°F/ Gas 2. Heat a medium, ungreased griddle or heavy-based frying pan over a moderate heat. Cook the tortillas, one at a time, for about 1½–2 minutes on each side. Turn over with a large palette knife when the bottom becomes a delicate brown. Adjust the heat if the tortilla browns too quickly.

5 Stack the flour tortillas in a clean tea cloth if you are eating them right away. Otherwise wrap in foil and keep them warm and soft in the preheated oven until you are ready to eat.

Quesadillas

These are delicious filled tortillas.

Makes 14

INGREDIENTS
14 freshly prepared unbaked tortillas

FOR THE FILLING
225 g/8 oz/1 cup finely chopped or
   grated Cheddar cheese
3 jalapeño chillies, seeded and cut into strips
salt
oil, for frying

1 Have the tortillas ready, covered
   with a cloth. Combine the cheese
and chilli strips in a bowl. Season
with salt. Set aside.

2 Heat the oil in a frying pan then,
   holding an unbaked tortilla on
your palm, put a spoonful of filling
along the centre, avoiding the edges.

3 Fold the tortilla and seal the edges
   by pressing well together. Fry on
both sides, until golden and crisp.

4 Remove the quesadilla and drain it
   on kitchen paper. Transfer to a
plate and keep warm while frying the
remaining quesadillas. Serve hot.

COOK'S TIP: For other stuffing
ideas try leftover beans with chillies,
or chopped chorizo sausage fried
with a little chopped onion.

Mixed Tostadas

These are like little edible plates.

Makes 14

INGREDIENTS
oil, for frying
14 freshly prepared unbaked corn tortillas
225 g/8 oz/1 cup mashed red kidney or
   pinto beans
1 iceberg lettuce, shredded
oil and vinegar dressing (optional)
2 cooked chicken breasts, skinned and
   thinly sliced
225 g/8 oz/1 cup guacamole
115 g/4 oz/1 cup coarsely grated
   Cheddar cheese
pickled jalapeño chillies, seeded and sliced,
   to taste, for garnish (optional)

1 Heat the oil in a frying pan and fry
   the tortillas until golden brown on
both sides and crisp, but not hard.

2 Spread each tortilla with a layer
   of beans. Put a layer of lettuce
(which can be lightly tossed with a
little dressing) over the beans.

3 Arrange pieces of chicken on the
   lettuce. Carefully spread over a layer
of the guacamole and finally sprinkle
over a layer of the grated cheese.

4 Arrange the mixed tostadas on a
   large platter. Serve on individual
plates but eat using your hands.

Right: Mixed Tostadas, Quesadillas.

Chimichangas

Chimichangas originally came from the state of Sonora.

Makes 14

INGREDIENTS
½ quantity Picadillo
14 freshly prepared unbaked flour tortillas
corn oil, for frying

TO GARNISH
whole radishes with leaves

1 Spoon about 60 ml/4 tbsp Picadillo down the centre of each tortilla. Fold in the sides, then the top and bottom, envelope-fashion, or simply roll up and fasten with a cocktail stick.

2 Pour the corn oil into a frying pan to a depth of about 2.5 cm/1 in. Set the pan over a moderate heat. Fry the chimichangas, a few at a time, for about 1–2 minutes, or until golden.

3 Drain on kitchen paper and keep warm. Serve the chimichangas garnished with whole radishes.

Tacos

The taco makes a great speedy snack to eat in your hand.

Makes as many as you like

INGREDIENTS
freshly prepared corn tortillas or
    pre-prepared taco shells

FOR THE FILLINGS
Picadillo topped with guacamole
chopped chorizo fried and mixed with
    chopped Cheddar cheese and chillies
Frijoles Refritos (Refried Beans) with
    sliced jalapeño chillies, guacamole,
    and cubed cheese
leftover Mole Poblano de Guajolote
    with guacamole
cooked chicken with salsa and lettuce

1 To make tacos, all you need is a supply of fresh corn tortillas, and as many of the suggested fillings as you can muster. Chillies and guacamole are always welcome, either in the taco or served as an extra on the side.

2 To make traditional soft tacos, simply spoon the filling on to the tortilla, wrap the tortilla around the filling – and eat.

3 To make hard tacos, secure the rolled up and filled tortilla with a cocktail stick, then briefly shallow fry until crisp and golden, or fill U-shaped taco shells with your chosen fillings.

Corn Soup

This is a simple-to-make yet very flavoursome soup. It is sometimes made with soured cream and cream cheese. Poblano chillies may be added.

Serves 4

INGREDIENTS

30 ml/2 tbsp corn oil
1 onion, finely chopped
1 red pepper, seeded and chopped
450 g/1 lb sweetcorn kernels,
    thawed if frozen
750 ml/1¼ pints/3 cups chicken stock
250 ml/8 fl oz/1 cup single cream
salt and freshly ground black pepper
½ red pepper, seeded and cut in
    small dice, to garnish

1 Heat the oil in a frying pan and sauté the onion and red pepper for about 5 minutes, until soft.

2 Add the sweetcorn and sauté for 2 minutes. Carefully tip the contents of the pan into a food processor or blender. Process until smooth, scraping down the sides and adding a little of the stock, if necessary.

3 Put the mixture into a saucepan and stir in the stock. Season to taste with salt and pepper, bring to a simmer and cook for 5 minutes.

4 Gently stir in the cream. Serve the soup hot or chilled, sprinkled with the diced red pepper. If serving hot, reheat gently after adding the cream, but do not allow the soup to boil.

Avocado Soup

This summery soup is very quick and easy to prepare and can be served hot or chilled.

Serves 4

INGREDIENTS
2 large ripe avocados
1 litre/1¾ pints/4 cups chicken stock
250 ml/8 fl oz/1 cup single cream
salt and freshly ground white pepper
15 ml/1 tbsp finely chopped coriander,
   to garnish (optional)

1 Cut the avocados in half lengthways, remove the stones and mash the flesh in the shells (see Cook's Tip). Put the mashed flesh into a strainer and, with a wooden spoon, press it through the strainer into a warm soup bowl.

2 Heat the chicken stock with the cream in a saucepan. When the mixture is hot, but not boiling, whisk it into the puréed avocado.

3 Season to taste with salt and pepper. Serve immediately, sprinkled with the coriander, if used. The soup may be served chilled, if you prefer.

COOK'S TIP: Mash the avocados in the shells by holding each half in the palm of one hand and mashing the flesh with a fork. This stops the avocado slithering about.

Red Snapper, Veracruz-style

This is Mexico's best-known fish dish. In Veracruz red snapper is always used but fillets of any firm-fleshed white fish can be substituted.

Serves 4

INGREDIENTS
4 large red snapper fillets
30 ml/2 tbsp freshly squeezed lime or
    lemon juice
120 ml/4 fl oz/½ cup olive oil
1 onion, finely chopped
2 garlic cloves, chopped
675 g/1½ lb tomatoes, peeled and chopped
1 bay leaf, plus a few sprigs to garnish
1.5 ml/¼ tsp dried oregano
30 ml/2 tbsp large capers,
    plus extra to serve (optional)
16 stoned green olives, halved
2 canned jalapeño chillies, drained,
    seeded and cut into strips
butter, for frying
3 slices firm white bread, cut into triangles
salt and freshly ground black pepper

2 Heat the oil in a large frying pan and sauté the onion and garlic until the onion is soft. Add the tomatoes and cook for about 10 minutes until the mixture is thick and flavoursome. Stir the mixture from time to time.

3 Stir in the bay leaf, oregano, capers, olives and chillies. Add the fish and cook over a very low heat for about 10 minutes or until tender.

1 Arrange the fish fillets in a single layer in a shallow dish. Season with salt and pepper, drizzle with the lime or lemon juice and set aside.

4 While the fish is cooking, heat the butter in a small frying pan and sauté the bread triangles until they are golden brown on both sides.

5 Transfer the cooked fish to a heated serving platter, pour over the tomato sauce and surround with the fried bread triangles. Garnish with sprigs of bay leaves and serve with extra capers, if you like.

COOK'S TIP: This can also be made with a whole fish, weighing about 1.5 kg/3–3½ lb. Bake with the sauce at 160°C/325°F/Gas 3. Allow 10 minutes for every 2.5 cm/ 1 in thickness of the fish.

Striped Bass in Sauce

This is a typically Mayan dish with its characteristic use of the spice *achiote* (annatto), which provides colour rather than flavour.

Serves 6

INGREDIENTS
1.5 kg/3–3½ lb striped bass or any
    non-oily white fish, cut into 6 steaks
120 ml/4 fl oz/½ cup corn oil
1 large onion, thinly sliced
2 garlic cloves, chopped
350 g/12 oz tomatoes, sliced
2 canned jalapeño chillies, rinsed,
    drained and sliced

FOR THE MARINADE
4 garlic cloves, crushed
5 ml/1 tsp black peppercorns
5 ml/1 tsp dried oregano
2.5 ml/½ tsp ground cumin
5 ml/1 tsp ground *achiote* (annatto)
2.5 ml/½ tsp ground cinnamon
120 ml/4 fl oz/½ cup mild
    white vinegar
salt
flat leaf parsley, to garnish

1 Arrange the fish steaks in a single layer in a shallow dish. Make the marinade. Using a pestle, grind the garlic and black peppercorns in a mortar. Add the dried oregano, cumin, *achiote* (annatto) and cinnamon and mix to a paste with the vinegar. Add salt to taste and spread the marinade on both sides of each of the fish steaks. Cover and leave in a cool place for 1 hour.

2 Select a flameproof dish large enough to hold the fish in a single layer and pour in enough of the oil to coat the base. Arrange the fish in the dish with any remaining marinade.

3 Top the fish with the onion, garlic, tomatoes and chillies and pour the rest of the oil over the top.

4 Cover the dish and cook over a low heat for 15–20 minutes, or until the fish is no longer translucent. Serve at once, garnished with the sprigs of flat leaf parsley.

Seviche

With the addition of sliced avocado, this would make a light summer lunch for four people.

Serves 6

INGREDIENTS
450 g/1 lb mackerel fillets,
    cut into 1 cm/½ in pieces
350 ml/12 fl oz/1½ cups freshly squeezed
    lime or lemon juice
225 g/8 oz tomatoes, chopped
1 small onion, very finely chopped
2 canned jalapeño chillies or 4 serrano
    chillies, rinsed, drained and chopped
60 ml/4 tbsp olive oil
2.5 ml/½ tsp dried oregano
30 ml/2 tbsp chopped fresh coriander
salt and freshly ground black pepper
lemon wedges and fresh coriander, to garnish
black and stuffed green olives, to serve

1 Put the fish into a glass dish and pour over the lime or lemon juice, making sure that the fish is completely covered. Cover and chill for 6 hours, turning once, by which time the fish will be opaque, "cooked" by the juice.

2 When the fish is opaque, lift it out of the juice with a slotted spoon, and set it aside, reserving the juice.

3 Combine the tomatoes, onion, chillies, olive oil, oregano and coriander in a bowl. Season to taste and pour in the reserved juice from the mackerel. Mix and pour over the fish.

4 Cover the dish and return the seviche to the fridge for about an hour to allow the flavours to blend. Seviche should not be served too cold. Allow it to stand at room temperature for 15 minutes before serving. Garnish with lemon wedges and coriander sprigs, serve with stuffed olives and sprinkled with chopped coriander.

COOK'S TIP: For a more delicately flavoured seviche, use a white fish such as sole or plaice.

Crab with Green Rice

For the best flavour, use fresh crab.

Serves 4

INGREDIENTS
225 g/8 oz/1 cup long grain rice
60 ml/4 tbsp olive oil
2 x 275 g/10 oz cans tomatillos
   (Mexican green tomatoes)
1 onion, chopped
2 garlic cloves, chopped
30 ml/2 tbsp chopped fresh coriander
about 350 ml/12 fl oz/1½ cups chicken stock
450 g/1 lb crab meat, thawed if frozen,
   broken into chunks
salt
chopped fresh coriander, to garnish
lettuce leaves, to serve

1 Soak the rice in hot water for 15 minutes, then drain. Heat the oil in a frying pan and sauté the rice, stirring until golden.

2 Drain the tomatillos, reserving the juice, and put them into a food processor. Add the onion, garlic and coriander, and process well. Pour into a measuring jug and add the juice. Pour in enough stock to make up to 475 ml/16 fl oz/2 cups and season.

3 Place the rice, tomato mixture and crab in a shallow pan. Cover and cook gently. Serve on lettuce leaves, garnished with fresh coriander.

Prawns with Pumpkin Seeds

A delicious summer lunch dish.

Serves 4

INGREDIENTS
175 g/6 oz/1 generous cup *pepitas*
   (Mexican pumpkin seeds)
450 g/1 lb raw prawns, thawed if frozen,
   peeled and deveined
1 onion, chopped
1 garlic clove, chopped
30 ml/2 tbsp chopped fresh coriander
225 g/8 oz tomatoes, peeled and chopped
1 canned jalapeño chilli, rinsed, drained,
   seeded and chopped
1 red pepper, seeded and chopped
30 ml/2 tbsp corn oil
salt
whole cooked prawns, lemon slices and
   fresh coriander sprigs, to garnish
rice, to serve

1 Grind the pumpkin seeds and shake through a strainer into a bowl.

2 Cook the prawns in boiling salted water. When pink, remove and set them aside. Reserve the cooking water.

3 Purée the onion, garlic, coriander, tomatoes, chilli, red pepper and pumpkin seeds in a food processor. Heat the oil and cook the mixture for 5 minutes. Season. Add prawn water to make a sauce, heat gently and add the prawns. Garnish and serve with rice.

Chicken in Green Almond Sauce

To add more colour, cut out the ribs from 2–3 outer leaves of a Cos lettuce, chop the leaves and add to the food processor.

Serves 6

INGREDIENTS
1.5 kg/3–3½ lb chicken,
    cut into serving pieces
475 ml/16 fl oz/2 cups
    chicken stock
1 onion, chopped
1 garlic clove, chopped
115 g/4 oz/2 cups fresh coriander,
    coarsely chopped
1 green pepper,
    seeded and chopped
1 jalapeño chilli, seeded and chopped
275 g/10 oz can tomatillos
    (Mexican green tomatoes)
115 g/4 oz/1 cup ground almonds
30 ml/2 tbsp corn oil
salt
fresh coriander, to garnish
rice, to serve

1 Put the chicken pieces into a flameproof casserole or shallow pan. Pour in the stock, bring to a simmer, cover and cook for about 45 minutes, until tender. Drain the stock into a measuring jug and set aside.

2 Put the onion, garlic, coriander, green pepper, chilli, tomatillos with their juice and the almonds in a food processor. Purée fairly coarsely.

3 Heat the oil in a frying pan, add the almond mixture and cook over a low heat, stirring with a wooden spoon, for 3–4 minutes. Scrape into the casserole or pan with the chicken.

4 Make the stock up to 475 ml/16 fl oz/2 cups with water, if necessary. Stir it into the casserole or pan. Mix gently and simmer just long enough to blend the flavours and heat the chicken through. Add salt to taste. Serve at once, garnished with coriander and accompanied by rice.

Mole Poblano de Guajolote

Mole Poblano de Guajolote is *the* great festive dish of Mexico for any special occasion or celebration.

Serves 6–8

INGREDIENTS
2.75–3.6 kg/6–8 lb turkey portions
1 onion, chopped
1 garlic clove, chopped
salt
90 ml/6 tbsp lard or corn oil
fresh coriander and roasted sesame
    seeds, to garnish

FOR THE SAUCE
6 dried ancho chillies, roasted and seeded
4 dried pasilla chillies, roasted and seeded
4 dried mulato chillies, roasted and seeded
1 canned chipotle chilli, drained,
    seeded and chopped (optional)
2 onions, chopped
2 garlic cloves, chopped
450 g/1 lb tomatoes,
    peeled and chopped
1 stale tortilla, torn into pieces
50 g/2 oz/⅓ cup seedless raisins
115 g/4 oz/1 cup ground almonds
45 ml/3 tbsp sesame seeds, ground
2.5 ml/½ tsp coriander seeds, ground
5 ml/1 tsp ground cinnamon
2.5 ml/½ tsp ground anise
1.5 ml/¼ tsp ground black peppercorns
60 g/4 tbsp lard or corn oil
40 g/1½ oz unsweetened
    (bitter) chocolate, broken into squares
15 ml/1 tbsp sugar
salt and freshly ground pepper
fresh coriander and sesame seeds, to garnish

1 Put the turkey into a saucepan in one layer. Add the onion and garlic, and cover with water. Season with salt, cover and simmer for about 1 hour, or until tender.

2 Tear the roasted chillies into pieces and put these into a small bowl. Cover with warm water and soak, turning occasionally for 30 minutes.

3 Lift out the turkey and pat dry with kitchen paper. Reserve the stock. Heat the lard or oil in a large frying pan and sauté the turkey until lightly browned all over. Transfer to a plate and set aside. Reserve the oil.

4 Tip the chillies and their water into a food processor. Add the chipotle chilli, if using, with the onions, garlic, tomatoes, tortilla, raisins, ground almonds, sesame seeds and spices. Process to a purée, in batches if necessary. Add the lard or oil to the fat in the frying pan. Heat, then add the chilli and spice paste. Cook, stirring, for 5 minutes.

5 Transfer the mixture to a saucepan. Stir in 475 ml/16 fl oz/2 cups of turkey stock (add water if necessary). Add the chocolate, and season. Cook over a low heat until the chocolate has melted. Stir in the sugar. Add the turkey and more stock if needed. Cover and simmer for 30 minutes. Garnish with fresh coriander and sprinkle with sesame seeds.

Pork with Pineapple

Adding fresh mint is the secret to this delicious variation of the classic combination of pork and pineapple.

Serves 6

INGREDIENTS
30 ml/2 tbsp corn oil
900 g/2 lb boneless pork shoulder or loin,
    cut into 5 cm/2 in cubes
1 onion, finely chopped
1 large red pepper,
    seeded and finely chopped
1 or more jalapeño chillies,
    seeded and finely chopped
450 g/1 lb fresh pineapple chunks
8 fresh mint leaves, chopped
250 ml/8 fl oz/1 cup chicken stock
salt and freshly ground black pepper
fresh mint sprig, to garnish
rice, to serve

2 Add the onion, red pepper and the chilli(es) to the frying pan. Sauté until the onion is tender, then add to the casserole with the pineapple. Stir to mix.

3 Add the mint and stock, cover and simmer gently for about 2 hours, or until the pork is tender. Garnish with fresh mint and serve with rice.

COOK'S TIP: If fresh pineapple is not available, use pineapple canned in its own juice.

1 Heat the oil in a large frying pan and sauté the pork in batches until the cubes are lightly coloured. Transfer the pork to a flameproof casserole.

Veal in Sauce

This is a delicate creamy dish.

Serves 6

INGREDIENTS
1.5 kg/3–3½ lb boneless veal,
    cut into 5 cm/2 inch cubes
2 onions, finely chopped
1 garlic clove, crushed
2.5 ml/½ tsp dried thyme
2.5 ml/½ tsp dried oregano
350 ml/12 fl oz/1½ cups chicken stock
75 g/3 oz/¾ cup very finely ground almonds,
    pecan nuts or peanuts
175 ml/6 fl oz/¾ cup soured cream
fresh oregano, to garnish
rice, to serve

1 Put the cubes of veal, onions, garlic, thyme, oregano and chicken stock into a large flameproof casserole. Bring to a gentle boil. Cover and simmer over a low heat for 2 hours, or until the veal is cooked and tender.

2 Put the nuts in a food processor. Pour in 120 ml/4 fl oz/½ cup of the veal liquid and process for a few seconds, until smooth. Press through a strainer into the casserole.

3 Stir in the soured cream and heat through gently, without boiling. Garnish with oregano and serve at once with the rice.

Opposite: Veal in Sauce, Picadillo.

Picadillo

Serves as a main dish with rice.

Serves 6

INGREDIENTS
30 ml/2 tbsp olive or corn oil
900 g/2 lb minced beef
1 onion, finely chopped
2 garlic cloves, chopped
2 eating apples, peeled, cored and chopped
450 g/1 lb tomatoes, peeled,
    seeded and chopped
2 or 3 pickled jalapeño chillies, drained,
    seeded and chopped
65 g/2½ oz/scant ½ cup raisins
1.5 ml/¼ tsp ground cinnamon
1.5 ml/¼ tsp ground cumin
salt and freshly ground black pepper
tortilla chips, to serve

TO GARNISH
15 g/½ oz/1 tbsp butter
25 g/1 oz/¼ cup slivered almonds

1 Heat the oil in a large frying pan and add the beef, onion and garlic and fry, stirring occasionally, until the beef is brown and the onion tender.

2 Add the apples to the pan with the remaining ingredients, except the garnish. Cook, uncovered, for about 20–25 minutes, stirring occasionally.

3 Make the garnish by melting the butter in a frying pan and sautéing the almonds until golden brown. Serve with tortilla chips.

Red Enchiladas

Dipping the tortillas in the sauce before cooking them in lard or oil produces a better flavour than frying them plain.

Serves 6

INGREDIENTS
4 dried ancho chillies, roasted and seeded
450 g/1 lb tomatoes, peeled,
   seeded and chopped
1 onion, finely chopped
1 garlic clove, chopped
15 ml/1 tbsp chopped fresh coriander
lard or corn oil, for frying
250 ml/8 fl oz/1 cup soured cream
4 chorizo sausages, skinned and chopped
18 freshly prepared unbaked corn tortillas
50 g/2 oz/2½ cups freshly grated
   Parmesan cheese
salt and freshly ground black pepper

3 Heat 15 ml/1 tbsp lard or oil in a frying pan. Add the purée and cook gently over a moderate heat, stirring, for 3–4 minutes. Season to taste with salt and pepper and then stir in the soured cream. Remove the pan from the heat and set aside.

4 Heat a further 15 ml/1 tbsp lard or oil in a small frying pan. Sauté the chorizo for a few minutes until lightly browned. Moisten with a little of the sauce and set the pan aside.

1 Tear the ancho chillies into pieces. Put in a bowl, add warm water to just cover, and soak for 20 minutes.

2 Tip the chillies, with a little of the soaking water, into a food processor. Add the tomatoes, onion, garlic and coriander and process.

5 Preheat the oven to 180°C/350°F/ Gas 4. Heat 30 ml/2 tbsp lard or oil in a frying pan. Dip a tortilla in the sauce and fry each side for a few seconds, shaking the pan gently.

6 Slide the tortilla on to a plate, top with some of the sausage mixture, and roll up. Pack the prepared tortillas in a single layer in a baking dish. Pour the sauce over, sprinkle with Parmesan and bake for about 20 minutes.

COOK'S TIP: If you prefer, fry the plain tortillas very quickly, then dip them in the sauce, stuff and roll. There is not a great loss of flavour, and no spatter.

37

Meat Balls

Mexican cooks use twice-minced beef and pork for *Albondigas*.

Serves 4

INGREDIENTS
225 g/8 oz lean minced beef
225 g/8 oz minced pork
50 g/2 oz/1 cup fresh
    white breadcrumbs
1 onion, finely chopped
2.5 ml/½ tsp dried oregano or
    ground cumin
salt and freshly ground black pepper
1 egg, lightly beaten
milk (optional)
corn oil, for frying
oregano leaves, to garnish

FOR THE SAUCE
beef stock
1 chipotle chilli, seeded and chopped
1 onion, finely chopped
2 garlic cloves, crushed
225 g/8 oz tomatoes, peeled,
    seeded and finely chopped

1 Put the minced beef and pork through a mincer or process in a food processor so that the mixture is finely minced. Tip it into a bowl and add the breadcrumbs, onion and oregano or cumin. Season with salt and pepper and stir in the egg.

2 Knead thoroughly to make a smooth mixture, adding a little milk if necessary. Shape the mixture into 4 cm/1½ in balls.

3 Heat 1 cm/½ in oil in a frying pan and fry the balls for 5 minutes, turning occasionally, until browned.

4 Put the meat balls in a flameproof casserole, cover with stock, add rest of sauce ingredients and simmer for about 30 minutes. Transfer the balls only to a serving dish. Strain the sauce and pour over. Garnish and serve.

COOK'S TIP: Alternatively, poach the meat balls in beef stock and add fresh tomato sauce to serve.

Frijoles

In the Yucatán peninsula in south-east Mexico, black haricot beans are cooked with the Mexican herb *epazote*.

Serves 6–8

INGREDIENTS
350 g/12 oz/1¼–1½ cups dried red kidney,
    pinto or black haricot beans,
    picked over and rinsed
2 onions, finely chopped
2 garlic cloves, chopped
1 bay leaf
1 or more serrano chillies
30 ml/2 tbsp corn oil
2 tomatoes, peeled, seeded and chopped
salt
sprigs of fresh bay leaves, to garnish

1 Put the dried beans into a large saucepan and add cold water to cover by 2.5 cm/1 in.

2 Add half the onion, half the garlic, the bay leaf and the chilli(es). Bring to the boil and boil vigorously for about 10 minutes. Put the beans and liquid into an earthenware pot or large saucepan, cover and cook over a low heat for 30 minutes. Add boiling water if the mixture starts to become dry.

3 When the beans begin to wrinkle, add 15 ml/1 tbsp of the corn oil and cook for a further 30 minutes or until the beans are tender. Add salt to taste and cook for 30 minutes more, but do not add any more water.

4 Remove the beans from the heat. Heat the remaining oil in a small frying pan and sauté the remaining onion and garlic until the onion is soft. Add the tomatoes and cook for a few minutes more.

5 Spoon 45ml/3 tbsp of the cooked beans out of the pot or pan and add them to the tomato mixture. Mash to a paste. Stir this into the remainder of the beans to thicken the liquid. Cook for just long enough to heat through, if necessary. Serve the beans in small bowls and garnish with sprigs of fresh bay leaves.

Mexican-style Rice

This colourful dish is garnished with attractive chilli "flowers" – warn everyone at the table that they will be hot.

Serves 6

INGREDIENTS
350 g/12 oz/1¾ cups long grain white rice
1 onion, chopped
2 garlic cloves, chopped
450 g/1 lb tomatoes, peeled, seeded and coarsely chopped
60 ml/4 tbsp corn or peanut oil
900 ml/1½ pints/3¾ cups vegetable stock
4–6 small red chillies
175 g/6 oz/1 cup cooked green peas
salt and freshly ground black pepper
fresh coriander sprigs, to garnish

3 Heat the oil in a large frying pan. Add the drained rice and sauté until it is golden brown. Using a slotted spoon, transfer the sautéed rice to a saucepan.

4 Reheat the oil remaining in the pan and cook the tomato purée for 2–3 minutes. Tip it into the saucepan and pour in the stock. Season to taste. Bring to the boil, reduce the heat to the lowest possible setting, cover the pan and cook for 15–20 minutes until almost all the liquid has been absorbed. Slice the red chillies from tip to stem end into four or five sections. Place in a bowl of iced water until they curl back to form flowers, then drain.

1 Soak the rice in a bowl of hot water for 15 minutes. Drain, rinse well under cold running water, drain again and set aside.

2 Combine the onion, garlic and tomatoes in a food processor and process to a purée.

5 Stir the peas into the rice mixture and cook, without a lid, until all the liquid has been absorbed and the rice is tender. Stir from time to time. Transfer to a serving dish and garnish with the drained chilli flowers and sprigs of coriander.

Chopped Courgettes

Calabacitas is an easy recipe. The acid in the tomatoes slows down the cooking of the courgettes.

Serves 4

INGREDIENTS
30 ml/2 tbsp corn oil
450 g/1 lb young courgettes, sliced
1 onion, finely chopped
2 garlic cloves, chopped
450 g/1 lb tomatoes, peeled,
   seeded and chopped
2 canned jalapeño chillies, rinsed,
   drained, seeded and chopped
15 ml/1 tbsp chopped fresh coriander
salt
fresh coriander, to garnish

1 Heat the oil in a flameproof casserole and add all the remaining ingredients, except the salt and the coriander.

2 Bring to simmering point, cover and cook over a low heat for about 30 minutes, until the courgettes are tender, checking from time to time that the dish is not drying out. If it is, add a little tomato juice, stock or water to the pan.

3 Season with salt and serve the Mexican way as a separate course. Garnish with fresh coriander.

Refried Beans
(Frijoles Refritos)

Refrito means twice fried, which to some cooks implies very well fried and to others twice cooked.

Serves 6–8

INGREDIENTS
90–120 ml/6–8 tbsp corn oil
1 onion, finely chopped
1 quantity *Frijoles* (cooked beans)

TO GARNISH
freshly grated Parmesan cheese or
   crumbled cottage cheese
crisp fried corn tortillas, cut into quarters

1 Heat 30 ml/2 tbsp of the oil in a large heavy-based frying pan and sauté the onion until it is soft. Add about 250 ml/8 fl oz/1 cup of the *Frijoles* (cooked beans).

2 Mash the beans with the back of a wooden spoon or potato masher, adding more beans and oil until all the ingredients are used up and the beans have formed a heavy paste. Use extra oil if necessary.

3 Tip out on to a warmed platter, piling the mixture up in a roll. Garnish with the cheese. Spike with the tortilla triangles, placing them at intervals along the length of the roll. Serve as a side dish.

Peppers Stuffed with Beans

On Independence Day in August, the green peppers are served with
a walnut sauce and a garnish of pomegranate seeds to represent
the colours of the Mexican flag.

Serves 6

INGREDIENTS
6 large green peppers
1 quantity Refried Beans
2 eggs, separated
2.5 ml/½ tsp salt
corn oil, for frying
plain flour, for dusting
120 ml/4 fl oz/½ cup
    whipping cream
115 g/4 oz/1 cup grated
    Cheddar cheese
fresh coriander sprigs,
    to garnish

1 Roast the peppers over a gas flame
or under a medium grill, turning
occasionally, until the skins have
blackened and blistered. Transfer the
peppers to a plastic bag, secure the top
and set aside for 15 minutes.

2 Preheat the oven to 180°C/350°F/
Gas 4. Remove the peppers from
the plastic bag. Hold each pepper in
turn under cold running water and
gently remove the skins by rubbing
them off. Slit the peppers down one
side and remove the seeds and ribs,
taking care not to break the pepper
shells. Stuff each pepper with the
Refried Beans.

3 Beat the egg whites in a large bowl
until they stand in firm peaks. In
another bowl, beat the yolks lightly
together with the salt. Fold the yolks
gently into the whites.

4 Pour the corn oil into a large
frying pan to a depth of about
2.5 cm/1 in and heat. Spread out the
flour in a shallow bowl or dish.

5 Dip the filled peppers in the flour
and then in the egg mixture. Fry in
batches in the hot oil until golden
brown all over. Arrange the peppers in
an ovenproof dish. Pour over the
cream and sprinkle with the cheese.
Bake in the oven for 30 minutes or
until the topping is golden brown
and the peppers are heated through.
Serve at once, garnished with fresh
coriander sprigs.

Green Lima Beans in Sauce

A colourful and tasty dish of lima beans with a tomato and chilli sauce.

Serves 4

INGREDIENTS
450 g/1 lb green lima or broad beans,
    thawed if frozen
30 ml/2 tbsp olive oil
1 onion, finely chopped
2 garlic cloves, chopped
350 g/12 oz tomatoes, peeled,
    seeded and chopped
1 or 2 canned jalapeño chillies, drained,
    seeded and chopped
salt
tortillas and chopped fresh coriander
    sprigs, to garnish

3 Add the jalapeño chilli(es) and continue to cook the mixture for 1–2 minutes, stirring frequently. Season with salt as desired.

1 Cook the beans in boiling water for 15–20 minutes, until tender. Drain and keep covered.

2 Heat the olive oil in a frying pan and sauté the onion and garlic until the onion is soft but not brown. Add the tomatoes and cook until the mixture is thick and flavoursome.

4 Pour the mixture over the reserved beans and check that they are hot. If not, return everything to the frying pan and cook over low heat for just long enough to heat through. Put into a warm serving dish, garnish with the tortillas and coriander and serve.

Green Bean & Sweet Red Pepper Salad

This multi-coloured salad – with a kick – is delicious served on its own or with other dishes at a summer dinner party.

Serves 4

INGREDIENTS
350 g/12 oz cooked green beans,
    quartered
2 red peppers, seeded and chopped
2 spring onions
    (white and green parts), chopped
1 or more drained pickled serrano chillies,
    well rinsed and then seeded
    and chopped
1 iceberg lettuce, coarsely shredded,
    or mixed salad leaves
olives, to garnish

FOR THE DRESSING
45 ml/3 tbsp red wine vinegar
120 ml/4 fl oz/ ½ cup olive oil
salt and freshly ground black pepper

1 Combine the green beans, red peppers, spring onions and chilli(es) in a salad bowl.

2 Make the salad dressing. Pour the red wine vinegar into a bowl or jug. Add salt and freshly ground black pepper to taste, then gradually whisk in the olive oil until well combined.

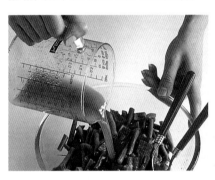

3 Pour the salad dressing over the prepared vegetables and toss lightly together to mix and coat thoroughly.

4 Line a large platter with the shredded lettuce leaves and arrange the salad attractively on top. Garnish with the olives and serve.

Avocado & Tomato Salad

The lemon juice helps prevent the avocados from discolouring.

Serves 4

INGREDIENTS
2 ripe avocados
2 large beefsteak tomatoes,
    about 225 g/8 oz each, peeled and seeded
1 iceberg lettuce, coarsely shredded
30 ml/2 tbsp chopped fresh coriander
salt and freshly ground black pepper

FOR THE DRESSING
90 ml/6 tbsp olive or corn oil
30 ml/2 tbsp fresh lemon juice

1 Cut the avocados in half, remove the stones and peel off the skin. Then cut the avocados and tomatoes lengthways into equal numbers of slices of approximately the same size.

2 Arrange a bed of shredded lettuce on a platter and place the tomato slices on top. Arrange the avocado slices over the tomato and sprinkle with coriander. Season to taste.

3 Whisk the olive or corn oil and lemon juice together in a jug until well combined.

4 Pour a little dressing over the salad and keep the rest aside to serve separately.

Chayote Salad

Chayote is also known as chocho, christophine and vegetable pear.

Serves 4

INGREDIENTS
2 chayotes, peeled and halved
1 large beefsteak tomato, about 225 g/8 oz,
    peeled and cut into 6 wedges
1 small onion, finely chopped
strips of seeded, pickled jalapeño chillies,
    to garnish

FOR THE DRESSING
2.5 ml/½ tsp Dijon mustard
30 ml/2 tbsp mild white vinegar
90 ml/6 tbsp olive or corn oil
salt and freshly ground black pepper

1 Cook the chayotes in a saucepan of boiling salted water for 20 minutes, or until tender. Drain and leave to cool. Remove the seeds. Cut the flesh into chunks about the same size as the tomatoes.

2 Make the dressing in a salad bowl. Combine the mustard and the vinegar with salt and pepper. Gradually whisk in the oil until well combined.

3 Put the chayote, tomato wedges and onion into a bowl. Add the dressing and toss gently together. Put in a serving dish, garnish with the chilli strips and serve.

Buñuelos

To save time, make the syrup in advance and chill until required, when it can be warmed through quickly.

Serves 6

INGREDIENTS
225 g/8 oz/2 cups plain flour
2.5 ml/½ tsp salt
5 ml/1 tsp baking powder
15 ml/1 tbsp sugar
1 large egg, beaten
120 ml/4 fl oz/½ cup milk
25 g/1 oz/2 tbsp unsalted butter,
   melted
oil, for frying
sugar, for dusting

FOR THE SYRUP
225 g/8 oz/1⅓ cups soft light brown sugar
750 ml/1¼ pints/3 cups water
2.5 cm/1 in cinnamon stick
1 clove

1 Make the syrup. Combine all the ingredients in a saucepan. Heat, stirring, until the sugar has dissolved, then simmer until the mixture has reduced to a light syrup. Remove and discard the spices. Keep the syrup warm while you make the *buñuelos*.

2 Sift the flour, salt and baking powder into a bowl. Stir in the sugar. In a separate mixing bowl, whisk the egg and the milk well together. Gradually stir in the dry mixture, then beat in the melted butter to make a soft dough.

3 Turn the dough on to a lightly floured board and knead until it is smooth and elastic. Divide the dough into 18 even-size pieces. Shape these pieces into balls. With your hands, flatten the balls to disk shapes about 2 cm/¾ in thick.

4 Use the floured handle of a wooden spoon to poke a hole through the centre of each *buñuelo*. Pour oil into a deep frying pan to a depth of 5 cm/2 in. Alternatively, use a deep-fryer. Heat the oil to a temperature of 190°C/375°F or until a cube of day-old bread browns in 30–60 seconds.

5 Add the *buñuelos* to the oil, frying in batches and taking care not to overcrowd the pan or deep-fryer. When the *buñuelos* are puffy and golden brown on both sides, lift them out with a slotted spoon and drain them thoroughly on kitchen paper. Dust the *buñuelos* with sugar, pour the warm syrup into a small bowl, and serve immediately.

Pumpkin in Brown Sugar

The best pumpkin to use for this recipe is the traditional orange-fleshed variety used to make Hallowe'en lanterns.

Serves 4

INGREDIENTS
900 g/2 lb pumpkin,
    cut into wedges
350 g/12 oz/2 cups soft dark brown sugar
about 120 ml/4 fl oz/½ cup water
natural yogurt and brown sugar,
    to serve (optional)

1 Scrape the seeds out of the pumpkin wedges. Pack the wedges firmly together in a heavy-based flameproof casserole.

2 Divide the sugar among the pumpkin pieces, packing it into the hollows which contained the seeds.

3 Pour the water carefully into the casserole to cover the bottom and prevent the pumpkin from burning. Take care not to dislodge the sugar when pouring in the water.

4 Cover and cook over a low heat, checking the water level frequently, until the pumpkin is tender and the sugar has dissolved to form a sauce.

5 Using a slotted spoon, transfer the pumpkin to a serving dish. Pour the sugary liquid from the pan over the pumpkin and serve at once with natural yogurt, sweetened with a little brown sugar, if you like.

Caramel Custards

This is a classic dessert in Mexico where it is known simply as *flan*.

Serves 6

INGREDIENTS
275 g/10 oz/1¼ cups granulated sugar
1 litre/1¾ pints/4 cups milk
6 eggs, lightly beaten
5 ml/1 tsp vanilla essence
pinch of salt

1 Preheat the oven to 180°C/350°F/ Gas 4. To make the caramel, put 115 g/4 oz/½ cup of the sugar into a small heavy-based saucepan. Heat, stirring constantly, until the sugar melts. Warm six ramekins by rinsing them in hot water and drying them quickly. Continue to heat the sugar syrup, without stirring, until it turns a deep golden colour. Remove the pan from the heat.

2 Pour some of the caramel into a ramekin and turn it so it coats the bottom and sides. As soon as the caramel sets, turn the ramekin upside down on a baking sheet. Coat the remaining ramekins in the same way.

3 Scald the milk by heating it in a saucepan to just below boiling point. Pour into a jug and cool.

4 Put the eggs into a bowl and gradually beat in the remaining sugar. Add the cooled milk, vanilla and salt. Mix together well. Strain the egg mixture into the ramekins and put them into a roasting tin filled with enough hot water to come halfway up the sides of the ramekins. Bake for about 40 minutes, or until a knife inserted in the centre of the custard comes out clean.

5 Cool the custards, then chill for several hours in the fridge. Wet a non-serrated knife and run it between the custards and the sides of the ramekins. Put a plate upside down over each ramekin and invert it quickly. The *flan* will easily slide out.

COOK'S TIP: Vary the flavour by adding a little ground cinnamon, cocoa or rum instead of vanilla.

Chocolate Corn Drink

This traditional drink is known in Mexico as *Champurrado*.

Serves 6

INGREDIENTS
50 g/2 oz/½ cup *masa harina*
   (tortilla flour)
750 ml/1¼ pints/3 cups
   water
5 cm/2 in cinnamon stick
750 ml/1¼ pints/3 cups milk
75 g/3 oz/3 squares Mexican chocolate,
   or any unsweetened
   (bitter) chocolate, grated
a little soft light brown sugar

1 Combine the *masa harina* and water in a large saucepan, stirring to mix well. Add the cinnamon stick and cook, stirring, over a low heat until the mixture has thickened.

2 Gradually stir in the milk, then the grated chocolate. Continue to cook until all the chocolate has dissolved. Discard the cinnamon stick and beat the liquid with a whisk or a Mexican *molinillo*. Sweeten to taste with brown sugar. Serve hot in cups.

COOK'S TIP: Unsweetened (bitter) chocolate can be used instead of Mexican. Add vanilla and almond essences, and cinnamon.

Mexican Hot Chocolate

In Mexico, hot chocolate is beaten with a pretty carved *molinillo*.

Serves 1

INGREDIENTS
250 ml/8 fl oz/1 cup water or milk
   or a mixture
40 g/1½ oz Mexican chocolate
   or any unsweetened (bitter) chocolate

1 Put the water or milk in a saucepan together with the chocolate and slowly bring to a simmer over a low heat. Simmer, stirring continuously, until the chocolate has melted. Continue to heat gently for 4–5 minutes to blend the flavours.

2 Pour the chocolate into a jug and beat with a Mexican *molinillo* until frothy. If a *molinillo* is not available, use a whisk or an electric mixer. Pour the chocolate into a mug and serve at once.

Bloody Maria

Tequila, made from the sap of blue agave, is named after the town that has made it for over 200 years.

Serves 2

INGREDIENTS
175 ml/6 fl oz/¾ cup tomato juice
90 ml/3 fl oz/6 tbsp white tequila
dash each of Worcestershire and
    Tabasco sauces
30 ml/2 tbsp lemon juice
salt and freshly ground black pepper
8 ice cubes

1 Combine the tomato juice, tequila, Worcestershire and Tabasco sauces, and lemon juice in a cocktail shaker. Add salt and pepper to taste, and four ice cubes. Shake very vigorously.

2 Place the remaining ice cubes in two heavy-based tumblers and strain the tequila mixture over them.

COOK'S TIP: When drinks are to be served with ice, make sure all the ingredients are thoroughly chilled ahead of time.

Margarita

The Margarita is undoubtedly the most popular and best-known cocktail made with tequila.

Serves 2

INGREDIENTS
½ lime or lemon
salt
120 ml/4 fl oz/½ cup white tequila
30 ml/2 tbsp Triple Sec or Cointreau
30 ml/2 tbsp freshly squeezed lime or
    lemon juice
4 or more ice cubes

1 Rub the rims of two cocktail glasses with the lime or lemon. Pour some salt into a saucer and dip the glasses in it to frost the rims.

2 Combine the tequila, Triple Sec or Cointreau, and lime or lemon juice in a tall glass container or jug and stir to mix well.

3 Pour the tequila mixture into the prepared glasses. Add the ice cubes and serve at once.

Index

The edition published by Hermes House

© Anness Publishing Limited 1999, updated 2001.

Hermes House is an imprint of Anness Publishing Limited,
Hermes House, 88–89 Blackfriars Road, London SE1 8HA

All rights reserved. No part of this publication may be reproduced, stored in a retrieval system,
or transmitted in any way or by any means, electronic, mechanical, photocopying, recording or otherwise,
without the prior written permission of the copyright holder.

Publisher: Joanna Lorenz

Editor: Valerie Ferguson

Series Designer: Bobbie Colgate Stone

Designer: Andrew Heath

Editorial Reader: Marian Wilson

Production Controller: Joanna King

Recipes contributed by: Elisabeth Lambert Ortiz

Photography: David Jordan

3 5 7 9 10 8 6 4 2

Notes:

For all recipes, quantities are given in both metric and imperial measures and, where appropriate, measures are also given in standard cups and spoons.
Follow one set, but not a mixture, because they are not interchangeable.

Standard spoon and cup measures are level.

1 tsp = 5 ml   1 tbsp =15 ml   1 cup = 250 ml/8 fl oz

Australian standard tablespoons are 20 ml.
Australian readers should use 3 tsp in place of 1 tbsp for measuring small quantities of gelatine, cornflour, salt, etc.

Medium eggs are used unless otherwise stated.

Printed in China